TWICE AS GOOD
Cookbook for Kids

by Hadley and Delaney

Be Safe and Sanitary In The Kitchen! Minors should ask an adult for assistance before attempting any recipe in this cookbook. Children should be supervised in the kitchen, particularly when using kitchen equipment and sharp utensils. Please wash your hands before handling all foods.

Recipes and Food Styling: Elizabeth Bouza
Photography: Karin Martinez (karinmartinez.com)
Logo and Branding: Audrey Denson (densondesign.com)
Graphic Design: Grace Delanoy (begraced.com)

Sales of the cookbook benefit the charitable organizations supported by the **Twice As Good Foundation**. Learn more at **www.twiceasgoodfoundation.org**.

ISBN: 978-0-9960696-0-1
Library of Congress Control Number: 2014936699
Manufactured in the United States of America
First printing: May, 2014

CONTENTS

Breakfast Time

Breakfast Flowers - 8

Mini Gooey Apple Cakes - 11

Olé! A Spanish Tortilla - 13

To-Go Breakfast Pastries - 15

Stuffed Apples - 19

Fruity Breakfast Lollipops - 21

Fun Snacks

Caramel Apples - 24

Crunchy Chickpeas - 27

Mountaintop Strawberries - 29

Chewy Fruity Squares - 30

Sticky Carrots - 33

Healthy Lunches

Baked Egg Rolls - 36

Vegetable Quiches - 39

BBQ at Lunchtime - 41

Pocket Chicken Salad - 42

Mix-It-Up Salad - 45

Veggie Quesadillas - 47

Family Dinners

Famous Star Ravioli - 50

My Little Roasted Hens - 53

Herby Salmon - 54

Chicken and Veggie Lasagna - 56

Slow Down for Gumbo - 59

Jar-It-Up Dressings

Zesty Mexican Vinaigrette - 60

Sunflower Power Vinaigrette - 62

Strawberry Field Dressing - 63

A Little Bit of Apricot - 64

A Touch of France Vinaigrette - 64

Asian Sensation - 65

Sweet Treats

Ice Cream Cone Cakes - 68

Banana Cupcakes - 72

Cheesecake Parfait - 75

Surprise Cookies - 77

Chocolate Peanut Butter Cups - 81

Superfood Combinations

Mango Magic Salad - 84

Crispy Kale - 85

Spectacular Spinach Salad - 86

WOW! Waldorf Salad - 87

Tasty Tomato Tart - 88

My Recipe! - 89

Index - 90

Recipe Index - 92

Kitchen Measurements - 93

Twice As Good Show - 94

Twice As Good Foundation - 95

Acknowledgements - 96

Dear Friends,

We hope you enjoy our new Twice as Good Cookbook! We wanted to share some yummy ways to make healthy eating lots of fun! For a recipe to be great it has to taste good and be good for you. We hope that you'll think that these recipes accomplish both goals!

For as long as we can remember, the kitchen has always been the loudest and most interesting room in the house. It seems like someone in our family is always making something delicious or creating something surprising. We try to be part of the fun by inventing our own dishes too!

Don't forget the first four rules of Kids' Cooking:

1. Wash your hands.
2. Ask an adult for help (especially with hot items, sharp utensils and appliances).
3. Don't be afraid to try new ingredients (especially if they are GREEN)!
4. Have fun!

We've divided our cookbook into seven sections: breakfast, lunch, dinner, snacks, desserts, salad dressings and superfood combinations. We hope it will be easy for you to find just the recipe that you're looking for. Our favorite section is the dressings because we L-O-V-E to experiment with different ingredients for our salads!

We hope your time in the kitchen with your family and friends is Twice as Good!

Hadley and Delaney

Breakfast Flowers

BREAKFAST TIME

Breakfast Flowers
Mini Gooey Apple Cakes
Olé! A Spanish Tortilla
To-Go Breakfast Pastries
Stuffed Apples
Fruity Breakfast Lollipops

Breakfast Flowers

PREP: 10 minutes
COOK: 15 minutes
SERVINGS: 6

Ingredients

nonstick cooking spray
6 slices of turkey bacon
6 slices of bread
½ cup grape tomatoes, cut in half
6 eggs
salt and pepper

Tools

muffin tin
1-inch round cookie cutter
cup
small shallow bowl
spoon

Step 1

Preheat the oven to 375°F. Spray the muffin tin
cups with nonstick cooking spray.

Step 2

Line the inside of each muffin cup with one slice
of turkey bacon, leaving a hole in the center.

Step 3

Use the round cookie cutter to cut out six circles
from each slice of bread.

Step 4
Put one circle on the bottom of each muffin cup and five on the sides to look like flower petals.

Step 5
Sprinkle a few tomatoes into each muffin cup.

Step 6
Crack the eggs one at a time into a small shallow bowl. Pour one egg into the center of each cup to make the "flowers."

Step 7
Season each flower with a pinch of salt and pepper.

Step 8
Bake the flowers for 15 minutes. Allow them to cool slightly, then use a spoon to remove them from the muffin cups. Enjoy your Breakfast Flowers!

Mini Gooey Apple Cakes

PREP: 15 minutes
COOK: 15 minutes
SERVINGS: 12 cakes

Ingredients

nonstick cooking spray
¾ cup maple syrup
½ cup pecans, whole
2 tablespoons pecans, chopped
1 tablespoon butter
1 teaspoon apple pie spice
2 medium Granny Smith apples, peeled
  and chopped
½ cup applesauce
1 egg
1 cup milk
2 teaspoons vanilla extract
1 cup packed brown sugar
¾ cup all-purpose flour
½ teaspoon baking soda
1 teaspoon baking powder
pinch of salt

Tools

12-cup muffin tin
sauté pan
spoons
mixing bowls
whisk
ladle
measuring spoons

Step 1
Preheat the oven to 425°F.
Spray the muffin cups with nonstick cooking spray.

Step 2
Add one tablespoon of maple syrup to each muffin cup, then sprinkle a few whole and chopped pecans over the maple syrup.

Step 3
Place the butter in a sauté pan over medium heat; carefully add the apple pie spice, apples and applesauce. Cook for 10 minutes while stirring. Spoon 2 tablespoons of the cooked apples into each muffin cup.

Step 4
Combine the egg, milk, vanilla extract and brown sugar in a mixing bowl and whisk until mixed well. Slowly whisk in the flour, baking soda, baking powder and salt.

Step 5
Ladle the batter ¾ of the way to the top of each muffin cup, covering the apples.

Step 6
Bake for 15 minutes. Allow the cakes to cool slightly before removing them from the muffin cups. Enjoy!

"Apples are our favorite snack!"

Olé! A Spanish Tortilla

PREP: 10 minutes
COOK: 45 minutes
SERVINGS: 8

Ingredients
nonstick cooking spray
2 cups of potatoes, grated
1 tablespoon olive oil
2 teaspoons paprika
8 eggs
¼ cup milk
½ teaspoon salt
¼ teaspoon pepper
½ cup grape tomatoes, sliced
½ cup chopped ham

Tools
9-inch cake pan
mixing bowls
whisk
measuring spoons
measuring cup

Step 1
Preheat the oven to 400°F. Spray a 9-inch cake pan with nonstick cooking spray.

Step 2
Mix together the grated potatoes, olive oil and paprika. Pour the potato mixture into the cake pan and form a crust by pressing the potatoes evenly on the bottom and up the sides of the pan, just like making a pie crust. Bake in the oven for 25 minutes.

Step 3
Meanwhile, mix the eggs, milk, salt and pepper in a mixing bowl until they are well incorporated.

Step 4
When the potato crust is ready, add the tomatoes and ham to the egg mixture and pour into the potato crust. Bake for 15-20 minutes or until the crust is golden brown.

Step 5
Remove from the oven, cut into wedges and serve. Enjoy!

Fun Fact! *There are 11 different vitamins and minerals in just one incredible egg!*

To-Go Breakfast Pastries

PREP: 45 minutes
COOK: 10 minutes
SERVINGS: 8

Ingredients

1 cup all-purpose or pastry flour
2 cups whole-wheat flour
4 tablespoons butter, cubed
½ cup ice-cold water
2 teaspoons sugar
1 teaspoon vanilla extract
¼ cup cornstarch
1 cup of your favorite jam
1 egg, beaten
¼ cup fun colorful sprinkles
1 cup powdered sugar
2 tablespoons milk

Tools

food processor   pastry brush
plastic wrap   measuring spoons
mixing bowls   measuring cup
rolling pin   ruler
pizza cutter
spoons
fork

Step 2
Place the lid on the food processor and mix by turning the food processor on and off for a few seconds at a time. Repeat until a big ball of dough is formed.

Step 3
Divide the dough into two equal parts and wrap each with plastic wrap. Let chill for 20 minutes.

Step 1
Place the two flours, butter, water, sugar and vanilla extract in the food processor.

15

To-Go Breakfast Pastries

Step 4

Preheat the oven to 375°F. Mix the cornstarch and your favorite jam together in a small bowl. Set it aside.

Step 5

20 minutes later...Now that the dough has chilled, use a rolling pin to roll it nice and thin, to about ¼ inch.

Step 6

Use a pizza cutter to make 8 even squares, then cut the squares in half to make 16 triangles.

Step 7

Place a teaspoon of the jam mixture in the center of eight of the dough triangles.

Step 8

Top them with the remaining eight triangles and seal all of the edges with a fork for a cute decoration.

Step 9

Brush all of the pastries with the beaten egg and bake for 10 minutes or until they are golden brown. Allow to cool for 10 minutes.

Step 10

Mix your sprinkles with the powdered sugar and milk to make a tie-dye frosting. Once the pastries are cooled, spread your fun frosting on each one and enjoy!

Stuffed Apples

PREP: 35 minutes
COOK: 15 minutes
SERVINGS: 8

Ingredients

8 small gala or red delicious apples
1 teaspoon cinnamon
½ cup packed brown sugar
½ cup peanut butter
1 cup yogurt
1 cup of your favorite granola

Tools

kid-friendly knife
melon baller
baking sheet
mixing bowls
spoon
measuring spoons
measuring cup

Step 1

Cut the tops off the apples and use a melon baller to scoop out all of the seeds, leaving a big enough pocket to stuff.

Step 2

Preheat the oven to 400°F. Combine the cinnamon and brown sugar in a mixing bowl. Rub the apples one at a time with the cinnamon-brown sugar mixture. Once they are coated, place the apples on a baking sheet and bake for 5 minutes.

Step 3

Combine the peanut butter and yogurt in a mixing bowl and mix until smooth.

Step 4

Fill the apples with the peanut butter and yogurt mixture. Decorate the tops with the granola. Bake for 10 minutes.

Step 5

Remove the apples from the oven and serve. Enjoy!

Fun Fact! *There are over 7,000 kinds of apples!*

Fruity Breakfast Lollipops

PREP: 15 minutes
COOK: 10 minutes
SERVINGS: 12 lollipops

Ingredients

nonstick cooking spray
1 cup all-purpose flour
1 teaspoon baking powder
1 cup milk
¼ cup sugar
2 eggs
1 teaspoon butter, melted
1 cup cream cheese, softened
1 cup mixed berries, chopped
lollipop sticks
½ cup maple syrup

Tools

2 large 1-inch-depth baking pans
Silpat or wax paper
blender
mixing bowl
mixing spoons
knife
measuring spoons
measuring cup

Step 1

Preheat the oven to 375°F. Evenly spray 2 large 1-inch-depth baking pans with nonstick cooking spray, and line each with a Silpat or wax paper.

Step 2

Combine the flour, baking powder, milk, sugar, eggs and butter in a blender container. Process until mixed. Pour this mixture into the two baking pans, equally divided. Shake the pans and make sure the mixture spreads evenly to each edge. Bake for 10 minutes. Allow the cakes to cool. Lift the cakes out of the pan and peel off the Silpat or wax paper.

Step 3

Combine the cream cheese and berries in a bowl and mix well.

Step 4

Gently spread some of the berry mixture on the two cakes. Once it's all spread out in an even layer, roll the cake to look like a log.

Step 5

Ask an adult to help cut the log into 2-inch pieces, then simply thread them onto your lollipop sticks.

Step 6

Drizzle the maple syrup on the lollipops and enjoy.

Fun Fact!

Maple syrup naturally contains potassium and calcium, making it a healthy way to sweeten up your breakfast.

Caramel Apples

FUN SNACKS

Caramel Apples
Crunchy Chickpeas
Mountaintop Strawberries
Chewy Fruity Squares
Sticky Carrots

Caramel Apples

PREP: 10 minutes
COOK: 2 minutes
SERVINGS: 4-6

Ingredients

3 Granny Smith apples
lollipop sticks
½ cup cream cheese
2 tablespoons maple syrup
½ cup butterscotch chips
½ cup chopped peanuts

Tools

melon baller
bowl or cup
rubber spatula
plate
measuring spoons
glass measuring cup

Step 1

Use a melon baller to make small round balls of apple (they do not have to be perfectly round).

Step 2

Thread each apple ball with a lollipop stick about halfway through the apple.

Step 3

Combine the cream cheese, maple syrup and butterscotch chips in a measuring cup. Melt in the microwave on High for 30-second intervals, stirring each time until the mixture is smooth.

Step 4

Dip each of the apples into the maple mixture until they are completely coated.

Step 5

Finally, simply dip the tips into the chopped nuts. Share and enjoy!

Crunchy Chickpeas

PREP: 5 minutes
COOK: 30 minutes
SERVINGS: 6

Ingredients

2 cups cooked chickpeas
3 teaspoons olive oil
1 teaspoon paprika
zest of 1 lemon
1 sprig fresh rosemary
½ cup Parmesan cheese, shaved

Tools

mixing bowl
zester
measuring spoons
measuring cup
baking sheet

Step 1
Preheat the oven to 350°F.

Step 2
Toss the chickpeas with the olive oil, paprika, lemon zest and rosemary sprig in a bowl. Spread on a baking sheet in a single layer.

Step 3
Bake for 15 minutes. Sprinkle with the Parmesan cheese and toss to mix. Bake for another 15 minutes.

Step 4
Remove the rosemary sprig, serve and enjoy.

Fun Fact! *Rosemary tea helps relieve headaches and toothaches.*

Mountaintop Strawberries

PREP: 10 minutes
SERVINGS: 6

Ingredients

12 large strawberries
¼ cup yogurt
½ cup blueberries
2 teaspoons mini chocolate chips
¼ cup shredded coconut

Tools

small spoon
mixing bowl
measuring spoons
measuring cup

Step 1

Use a small spoon to hollow out the center of each strawberry.

Step 2

Mix together the yogurt and blueberries in a bowl, crushing some of the berries with the back of a spoon. Add the mini chocolate chips.

Step 3

Stuff each of the strawberries with a spoonful of the yogurt mixture and top each with shredded coconut.

Fun Fact!

Blueberries, strawberries, and chocolate are all packed with nutritious ANTIOXIDANTS, making this a SUPER SNACK!

Chewy Fruity Squares

PREP: 5 minutes
COOK: 2-2½ hours
SERVINGS: 6

Ingredients

1 cup peaches, peeled and sliced
2 cups blueberries
½ cup applesauce
2 teaspoons honey

Tools

blender
rubber spatula
cookie sheet
Silpat or wax paper
scissors
measuring spoons
measuring cup

Step 1

Preheat the oven to 150°F.

Step 3

Line a cookie sheet with a Silpat or wax paper and spread the fruit purée evenly from edge to edge.

Step 2

Place all of the ingredients in a blender and purée.

Step 4

Bake for 2-2½ hours. When done, it will be dry but very flexible.

Step 5

When ready, transfer the dried fruit onto two pieces of wax paper. Use kid-safe scissors to cut the dried fruit into long, thin strips or squares. Line them with baking parchment paper and keep for up to two weeks in an airtight container.

31

Sticky Carrots

PREP: 5 minutes
COOK: 20 minutes
SERVINGS: 4-6

Ingredients

½ cup honey
2 tablespoons soy sauce
1 tablespoon miso paste
1 tablespoon grated ginger
1 teaspoon mixed black and white sesame
   seeds
3 cups baby carrots

Tools

mixing bowl
spoon
baking dish
measuring spoons
measuring cup

Step 1
Preheat the oven to 400°F.

Step 2
Combine the honey, soy sauce, miso paste, ginger and sesame seeds in a large bowl and mix well with a spoon.

Step 3
Toss in the carrots and be sure to stir to completely coat all of them in your sticky mixture.

Step 4
Lay the carrots in a baking dish in a single layer.

Step 5
Bake for 10 minutes. Remove from the oven. Stir and toss to coat. Bake for another 10 minutes.

Step 6
Enjoy!

Fun Fact! *Carrots are a "root vegetable," meaning the edible part grows completely underground.*

Baked Egg Rolls

HEALTHY LUNCHES

Baked Egg Rolls
Vegetable Quiches
BBQ at Lunchtime
Pocket Chicken Salad
Mix-It-Up Salad
Veggie Quesadillas

Baked Egg Rolls

PREP: 20 minutes
COOK: 10-12 minutes
SERVINGS: 8

Ingredients

1 cup cooked chicken, shredded
½ cup finely grated carrots
½ cup water chestnuts, finely chopped (optional)
½ cup bean sprouts
2 green onions, chopped
1 teaspoon ginger powder
1 tablespoon cornstarch
3 tablespoons soy sauce
1 tablespoon cilantro, chopped
8 egg roll wrappers
1 cup water
cooking spray

Tools

mixing bowl
spatula
measuring spoons
measuring cup
baking sheet

Step 1

Preheat the oven to 400°F.

Step 2

Mix together the chicken and all of the vegetables in a bowl.

Step 3

Combine the ginger powder, cornstarch, soy sauce and cilantro in a small bowl. Pour over the chicken mixture and toss until mixed well.

Step 4

Lay one egg roll wrapper on a flat surface and put two spoonfuls of the mixture on the bottom corner of the wrapper.

Step 5
Brush the outer edges with water.

Step 6
Fold the bottom tip to the center over the filling.

Step 7
Bring the outer edges to the center and roll forward tightly. Repeat steps 4-7 for all of the wrappers to make 8 eggrolls.

Step 8
Lay all of the egg rolls on a baking sheet and spray with cooking spray. Bake for 10-12 minutes or until the edges are a nice golden brown.

Vegetable Quiches

PREP: 15 minutes
COOK: 25 minutes
SERVINGS: 6-8

Ingredients

Crust:
nonstick cooking spray
2 cups whole-wheat crackers
1 teaspoon thyme
2 tablespoons olive oil
1 teaspoon garlic powder

Filling:
1 teaspoon olive oil
1 portabella mushroom, chopped into
   small pieces
1 zucchini, chopped
1 cup spinach, chopped
½ cup grape tomatoes, chopped
4 eggs
5 egg whites
¼ cup milk
¼ cup feta cheese

Tools

12-cup muffin tin
sauté pan
spatula
mixing bowl
whisk

Step 1
Preheat the oven to 350°F. Spray the muffin cups with nonstick cooking spray.

Step 2
Place the crackers, thyme, olive oil and garlic powder in a food processor and mix by turning the processor on and off for a few seconds at a time. Repeat until the crackers are chopped and the mixture looks like "wet sand."

Step 3
Press about two tablespoons of the "wet sand" into each muffin cup and form a crust by firmly pressing it into the cups. Bake for 10-15 minutes or until light golden brown.

Step 4
While the crusts are baking, heat the olive oil in a sauté pan and cook the mushroom and zucchini in the oil until they are tender. Add the spinach and tomatoes. Remove from the heat and allow to cool.

Step 5
Combine the eggs, egg whites, milk and feta cheese in a large bowl and whisk until mixed well. Add the cooled vegetables to the egg mixture and spoon into each baked crust ¾ of the way to the top. Bake for 15 minutes and enjoy!

BBQ at Lunchtime

PREP: 5 minutes
COOK: 15 minutes
SERVINGS: 4

Ingredients

1 cup tomato sauce
½ cup apple juice
1 can pineapple chunks, drained
1 teaspoon onion powder
1 teaspoon garlic powder
½ teaspoon mustard powder
1 teaspoon salt
2 cups roasted chicken, shredded
shredded lettuce
sliced tomato
4 sandwich buns, toasted

Tools

small saucepot
rubber spatula
measuring spoons
measuring cup

Step 1

To make the barbeque sauce, combine the tomato sauce, apple juice, pineapple, onion powder, garlic powder, mustard and salt in a saucepot and cook over medium heat for 10 minutes.

Step 2

Stir the shredded chicken into the barbeque sauce and cook for an additional 5 minutes or until the chicken is heated through.

Step 3

Assemble the sandwiches by layering the bottom of each bun with slices of tomato and about ¼ of the barbeque chicken. Top with shredded lettuce and finish with a bun. Enjoy!

Fun Fact !

There are at least 10 different spellings or nicknames for BBQ: barbeque, barbecue, Bar-B-Cue, Bar-B-Que, Bar-B-Q, and 'Cue, 'Que, Barbie and Q!

Pocket Chicken Salad

PREP: 10 minutes
SERVINGS: 4

Ingredients

1 cup shredded carrots
2 tablespoons olive oil
2 tablespoons soy sauce
2 cups roasted chicken, shredded
2 tablespoons raisins
1 cup shredded lettuce
salt and pepper
2 pitas, cut into quarters
1 tomato, sliced

Tools

mini food processor
mixing bowl
spoon
measuring spoon
measuring cup

Step 1

Place the carrots, olive oil and soy sauce in a mini food processor. Process for a few seconds at a time, repeating until mixed well.

Step 2

Add the carrot mixture to the chicken in a bowl. Toss in the raisins and shredded lettuce. Season your salad with a pinch of salt and pepper.

Step 3

Open the pitas to make a pocket in each one. Place a few tomato slices in each pita pocket followed by ¼ cup chicken salad. Serve cold.

Mix-It-Up Salad

PREP: 10 minutes
SERVINGS: 4

Ingredients
4 resealable bags
1 cup roasted chicken breast, diced
½ cup carrots, sliced
½ cup grape tomatoes, halved
½ pear, sliced
2 teaspoons lemon juice
½ cup sliced almonds
3 cups chopped romaine lettuce
1 cup of your favorite dressing

Tools
plate
fork
measuring cup
measuring spoons

Step 1
Open all of the bags and place ¼ cup chicken in each.

Step 2
Follow with a layer of carrots and tomatoes in each bag.

Step 3
Toss the pear in the lemon juice. Removed and place a few slices in each bag.

Step 4
Finish with a sprinkle of almonds and top with romaine lettuce. Seal the bag tightly! Pack in a lunch box along with a ¼ cup of your favorite dressing (carefully sealed in a separate container.)

Step 5
When ready for lunch, open each bag and pour your dressing right on top. Carefully close the bag once more and shake to mix. Make sure all of the ingredients are covered with the yummy dressing.

Step 6
Simply pour the salad onto plates and enjoy!

Veggie Quesadillas

PREP: 10 minutes
COOK: 15 minutes
SERVINGS: 4

Ingredients

1 teaspoon olive oil
½ cup broccoli florets, chopped
1 red bell pepper, seeded and diced
1 cup spinach leaves
1 teaspoon fajita seasoning
salt and pepper
2 large spinach wraps
1 cup shredded mozzarella cheese
1 cup of your favorite salsa

Tools

2 nonstick sauté pans
large spatula
kid-friendly knife

Step 1

Heat a sauté pan over medium-low and then pour in the olive oil. Slowly add the broccoli and red bell pepper. Cook and stir for about 4 minutes.

Step 2

Next add the spinach, fajita seasoning and a pinch of salt and pepper. Cook for another minute, then remove from the heat and set it aside.

Step 3

To assemble the veggie quesadillas, place each spinach wrap down on a clean flat surface. On one side of the wrap sprinkle half of the cheese. Cover the cheese with the cooked vegetables and top with the remaining cheese. Fold over each wrap to look like a half circle.

Step 4

Heat a nonstick sauté pan over medium heat and cook each veggie quesadilla for 4-5 minutes per side.

Step 5

Slice into triangles and top with your favorite salsa.

Step 6

Enjoy!

Fun Fact ! *Cooking spinach actually increases its health benefits...wow!*

Famous Star Ravioli

FAMILY DINNERS

Famous Star Ravioli
My Little Roasted Hens
Herby Salmon
Chicken and Veggie Lasagna
Slow Down for Gumbo

Famous Star Ravioli

PREP: 30 minutes
COOK: 15 minutes
SERVINGS: 4-6

Ingredients
1 package of wonton wrappers
1 cup water

Filling
½ cup ricotta cheese
¼ pound ground chicken
½ cup basil, chopped
¼ cup pine nuts
½ cup Parmesan cheese
1 egg
1 pinch nutmeg
1 teaspoon salt
1 teaspoon pepper

Sauce
3 teaspoons olive oil
1 clove garlic, minced
2 cups grape tomatoes, sliced
salt and pepper

Tools
mixing bowl
star-shaped cookie cutter
large pot
sauté pan
spoons

Step 1
Combine the ingredients for the filling in a large bowl, stirring until mixed well.

Step 2
Lay out a few wonton wrappers in a straight line, keeping the rest covered with a damp towel.

Step 6

Use a star-shaped cookie cutter to cut the wonton wrappers. Repeat until you've used all of your wrappers.

Step 3

Spoon a teaspoon of your filling onto the center of the wonton wrapper.

Step 7

Ask your adult helper to cook the ravioli by gently placing them in boiling water. Allow the ravioli to cook for a total of 8 minutes. Once they are cooked, gently remove them from the water and arrange them on a platter.

Step 4

Dip your finger in the water and wet all edges of the wonton wrapper.

Step 8

Heat the olive oil in a large skillet and add the garlic, tomatoes and a pinch of salt and pepper. Cook while stirring gently for 5 minutes. Place the warm tomatoes on top of the cooked raviolis and enjoy!

Step 5

Carefully place another wonton wrapper on top and press the edges together to make a nice seal.

My Little Roasted Hens

PREP: 15 minutes
COOK: 35 minutes
SERVINGS: 4

Ingredients

1 cup chopped onion
2 cups chopped celery
¼ cup olive oil
1 teaspoon paprika
2 teaspoons salt
1 teaspoon black pepper
2 tablespoons ketchup
4 Cornish game hens

Stuffing:

2 cups cooked rainbow quinoa
1 apple, diced
½ cup cranberries
½ cup chicken stock
½ cup chopped parsley
¼ cup pine nuts
¼ teaspoon nutmeg
salt and pepper

Tools

roasting pan
mixing bowl
spoon
pastry brush
kitchen twine

Step 1
Preheat the oven to 375°F. Prepare a roasting pan by putting a layer of the onion and celery at the bottom.

Step 2
Combine the olive oil, paprika, salt, pepper and ketchup in a bowl.

Step 3
Brush some of the seasoned oil all over each hen. Don't forget the inside!

Step 4
Mix the stuffing ingredients in a bowl.

Step 5
Spoon the stuffing mixture into each hen, making sure each one gets an equal portion.

Step 6
Using the kitchen twine, tie the legs of the hens together tightly in order to keep the stuffing inside.

Step 7
Place the hens over the onion and celery in the roasting pan.

Step 8
Place the hens in the oven and roast for 35 minutes.

Fun Fact! *Quinoa is pronounced "KEEN-wah."*

Herby Salmon

Step 1
Preheat the oven to 400°F.

Step 2
Mix the olive oil and lemon juice and pour over the salmon in a shallow bowl.

Step 3
Mix the parsley, tarragon, lemon zest, salt and lemon pepper seasoning in a mixing bowl.

PREP: 10 minutes
COOK: 8 minutes
SERVINGS: 4

Ingredients
¼ cup olive oil
juice of 1 lemon
4 salmon fillets, cut into cubes
½ cup fresh parsley, chopped
½ cup fresh tarragon, chopped
zest of 1 lemon
1 teaspoon salt
1 teaspoon lemon pepper seasoning
1 leek, sliced thin

Tools
mixing bowl
roasting dish
spoon

Step 4
Place the sliced leek in the roasting dish. Dip the salmon cubes in the herbs to make a nice crust, then place on top of the leek.

Step 5
Bake the salmon for 8 minutes.

Chicken and Veggie Lasagna

Ingredients

¼ cup olive oil
½ lb. chicken breast, diced
1 onion, diced
1 teaspoon garlic, minced
1 zucchini, chopped small
1 yellow squash, chopped small
1 eggplant, chopped small
1 can crushed tomatoes
1 cup chicken stock
1 teaspoon sugar
salt and pepper
1 package no-boil lasagna noodles
1 cup shredded mozzarella cheese
1 cup ricotta cheese
1 cup fresh basil leaves

PREP: 15 minutes
COOK: 1 hour
SERVINGS: 4-6

Tools

lasagna dish or casserole dish
large saucepot
spoons

Step 1

Heat the olive oil in a large saucepot over medium heat. Lightly brown the chicken in the hot oil.

Step 2

Add the diced onion and garlic and cook until the onion is translucent.

Step 3

Next, add the zucchini, squash and eggplant to the onion and garlic. Continue to cook for an additional 5 minutes, stirring occasionally.

Step 4

Add the crushed tomatoes, chicken stock and sugar. Season with a pinch of salt and pepper. Cover and cook for 10 minutes.

Step 5

Finally, it's time to assemble your lasagna! But first, preheat your oven to 375°F.

Step 6

Place a small spoonful of sauce on the bottom of your baking dish. Follow with a layer of the lasagna noodles (using ⅓ of the noodles.)

Step 7

Spoon half of your sauce on top of the noodles, followed by a sprinkle of mozzarella cheese.

Step 8

Add a layer of ricotta cheese, then top with a layer of noodles.

Step 9

Repeat Step 7.

Step 10

Add a final layer of noodles followed by a layer of basil leaves. Finish with a nice sprinkle of mozzarella cheese. Cover with foil.

Step 11

Bake for 30 minutes covered, then for 10 minutes uncovered. Allow to rest 10 minutes before cutting. Enjoy!

Slow Down for Gumbo

PREP: 10 minutes
COOK: 4 hours, 20 minutes
SERVINGS: 4-6

Ingredients

1 pound chicken thighs
½ pound andouille sausage, sliced
1 onion, chopped
2 stalks celery, chopped
1 green bell pepper, seeded and chopped
1 cup corn kernels
2 cups frozen okra
2 cups chicken stock
1 can crushed tomatoes
1 tablespoon Old Bay seasoning
1 teaspoon salt
1 teaspoon pepper
1 teaspoon garlic powder
1 teaspoon cumin
½ pound shrimp

Tools

slow cooker
measuring spoons
measuring cup

Step 1

Combine all of the ingredients except for the shrimp in a slow cooker.

Step 2

Set the slow cooker to cook on low for 4 hours.

Step 3

After 4 hours, add the shrimp and set the slow cooker to cook for an additional 20 minutes.

Step 4

Serve and enjoy!

Fun Fact!

"Gumbo" is actually another name for the vegetable okra.

Zesty Mexican Vinaigrette

Tools
jar with lid
measuring spoons
measuring cup

Ingredients
½ cup olive oil
¼ cup rice wine vinegar
¼ cup chopped cilantro
2 tablespoons honey

Instructions
Place all ingredients in a jar,
put the lid on the jar
and give it a
shake, shake, shake!

60

JAR-IT-UP DRESSINGS

Zesty Mexican Vinaigrette

Sunflower Power Dressing

Strawberry Field Dressing

A Little Bit of Apricot

A Touch of France Vinaigrette

Asian Sensation

Jar-It-Up Dressings

PREP: 5 minutes
SERVINGS: 4-6

Each dressing can be used for your favorite salad combination.

Tools
jar with lid
measuring spoons
measuring cup

Instructions for ALL Jar-It-Up Dressings
Place all ingredients in a jar, put the lid on the jar then give it a *shake, shake, shake*!

Sunflower Power Vinaigrette

Ingredients
½ cup sunflower oil
½ teaspoon mustard powder
¼ cup champagne vinegar
½ teaspoon chopped thyme
1 tablespoon honey
pinch of salt

Fun Fact!

Sunflower oil is only made from black sunflower seeds.

Strawberry Field Dressing

Ingredients:
½ cup olive oil
¼ cup balsamic vinegar
4 strawberries, chopped
1 tablespoon strawberry jam
1 teaspoon salt
½ teaspoon pepper

A Little Bit of Apricot

Ingredients
½ cup walnut oil
2 tablespoons apricot preserves
¼ cup sherry vinegar
1 teaspoon chopped basil
pinch of salt and pepper

A Touch of France Vinaigrette

Ingredients
½ cup olive oil
¼ cup red wine vinegar
3 tablespoons Dijon mustard
1 tablespoon honey
1 teaspoon chopped shallots
pinch of salt and pepper

Instructions for ALL Jar-It-Up Dressings
Place all ingredients in a jar, put the lid on the jar then give it a *shake, shake, shake*!

Asian Sensation

Ingredients

1 teaspoon brown sugar
1 teaspoon sesame oil
½ cup canola oil
1 lemon, juiced
¼ cup ponzu sauce

Ice Cream Cone Cakes

SWEET TREATS

Ice Cream Cone Cakes
Banana Cupcakes
Cheesecake Parfait
Surprise Cookies
Chocolate Peanut Butter Cups

Ice Cream Cone Cakes

Step 1

Preheat the oven to 350°F. Cover the cake pan top with three layers of aluminum foil. Make 24 pin-size holes 2 inches apart using a wooden skewer. Set it aside.

PREP: 15 minutes
COOK: 15-20 minutes
SERVINGS: 24 cones

Ingredients

24 mini ice cream cones
1½ cups all-purpose flour
2 teaspoons baking powder
1 teaspoon baking soda
pinch of salt
1 egg
1 cup applesauce
¼ cup milk
¼ cup vegetable oil
¼ cup packed brown sugar
1 cup of your favorite frosting
24 cherries

Tools

aluminum foil
deep cake pan
wooden skewer
mixing bowl
mixing spoons

Step 2

Place the tips of each ice cream cone in the pin-size holes in the aluminum foil. Gently press down.

Tip! *Press the cone gently and try to keep it standing straight up.*

Step 3

Combine the flour, baking powder, baking soda and salt in a mixing bowl.

Step 4

Mix together the egg, applesauce, milk, vegetable oil and brown sugar in a bowl using a whisk.

Step 5

Slowly add the flour mixture to the applesauce mixture.

Step 6

Fill each ice cream cone with the cake batter ¾ of the way to the top. Bake for 15 minutes. Let cool.

Step 7

Decorate the cooled ice cream cone cakes with scoops of your favorite frosting and decorations! Yum!

Fun Fact! *An average cherry tree can grow 7,000 cherries each year!*

Banana Cupcakes

PREP: 15 minutes
COOK: 12 minutes
SERVINGS: 12 cupcakes

Tools

12-cup muffin tin
paper cupcake liners
measuring spoons
measuring cups
mixing bowl
flour sifter or strainer
fork
hand mixer
spoon
cake tester

Ingredients

1½ cups cake flour
1 teaspoon baking soda
½ teaspoon baking powder
2 ripe bananas
½ cup packed brown sugar
1 egg
¼ cup milk
¼ cup vegetable oil
½ cup butterscotch chips
decorative sprinkles

Frosting

1 cup whipped cream cheese
½ cup powdered sugar
1 teaspoon pumpkin pie spice
1 teaspoon vanilla extract

Step 1

Preheat the oven to 350°F. Prepare a 12-cup muffin tin by placing a paper cupcake liner in each cup.

Step 2

Sift the flour, baking soda and baking powder together, then set aside.

Step 3

Place the bananas in a large bowl and use a fork to mash them.

Step 4

Carefully mix the brown sugar, egg, milk and oil with the bananas using a hand mixer set on low.

Step 5

Gently fold the flour mixture and butterscotch chips into the banana mixture.

Step 6

Fill your cupcake liners ¾ of the way to the top.

Step 7

Bake the cupcakes for 10-12 minutes, or until the cupcakes test done. Let cool.

Step 8

Mix all of the frosting ingredients together in a mixing bowl using a hand mixer on medium-low.

Step 9

Decorate the cooled cupcakes with the frosting and your favorite decorative sprinkles. Enjoy!

Cheesecake Parfait

PREP: 15 minutes
SERVINGS: 4

Ingredients

1 cup pretzels
1 cup toasted pecans
½ cup mini white chocolate chips
1 (8-oz.) package light cream cheese,
    softened
1 teaspoon vanilla extract
½ teaspoon almond extract
1 cup blueberries in syrup
1 cup whipped cream
pretzels

Tools

kid-friendly food processor
mixing bowl
hand mixer
rubber spatula

Step 1

Place 1 cup pretzels, pecans and white chocolate chips in a food processor. Process for a few seconds at a time, repeating until well mixed.

Step 2

Place two spoonfuls of the crushed nut mixture in each of your parfait glasses.

Step 3

Use a hand mixer to whip the cream cheese, vanilla extract, almond extract and blueberries in a bowl until light and fluffy.

Step 4

Lightly fold half of the cream cheese mixture into the blueberry cream cheese mixture with a rubber spatula to make a blueberry mousse.

Step 5

Spoon a layer of the whipped cream mixture and a layer of blueberry mousse over the crushed nuts in your parfait glasses. Top with the remaining whipped cream and a few extra pretzels. Enjoy!

Fun Fact !

Blueberries are a yummy brain food that help to keep you focused!

Surprise Cookies

PREP: 1 hour, 30 minutes
COOK: 10 minutes
SERVINGS: 2 dozen

Ingredients
2½ cups whole-wheat flour
2 teaspoons cream of tartar
1 teaspoon baking soda
1 teaspoon salt
1 teaspoon ground ginger
1 teaspoon cinnamon
½ cup packed brown sugar
½ cup butter, softened
2 eggs
1 teaspoon vanilla extract
12 store-bought square caramels,
　　unwrapped and cut in half
½ cup granulated sugar
2 tablespoons cinnamon

Tools
hand mixer
flour sifter or strainer
measuring spoons
measuring cup
mixing bowls
whisk
ice cream scooper
cookie sheet

Step 1
Sift the flour, cream of tartar, baking soda, salt,
ginger and 1 teaspoon cinnamon together.

Step 2
Combine the brown sugar, butter, eggs and
vanilla extract in a bowl and mix well.

Step 3

Slowly add the flour mixture to the brown sugar mixture, stirring after each addition.

Step 4

Use an ice cream scooper to scoop the cookie dough onto a cookie sheet.

Step 5

Make a hole in the center of the cookie dough with your finger and stuff it with a piece of caramel. Reseal it to look like a round ball again. Repeat this step for the rest of the scooped cookie dough. Once done, place them in the freezer for 10 minutes.

Step 6
Preheat the oven to 375°F.
Meanwhile, mix the granulated sugar and
2 tablespoons cinnamon together in a bowl.

Step 7
Slightly flatten and roll each of the chilled dough
balls in the cinnamon-sugar. Once coated, place
onto a cookie sheet. Bake for 8-10 minutes or
until light golden brown. Cool before eating!

Quick Tip!

*Sifting flour prevents
lumps in your dough
and makes your
cookies light as air!*

Chocolate Peanut Butter Cups

PREP: 25 minutes
SERVINGS: 1 dozen

Ingredients

1 sleeve chocolate graham crackers
¼ cup butter, melted
¼ cup light whipped cream cheese
½ cup peanut butter
1 cup powdered sugar
1 cup chocolate chips, melted

Tools

large resealable bag
rolling pin
mixing bowls
spoons
mini muffin tin
piping bag

Fun Fact !

To make just one pound of chocolate, you need approximately 400 cacao beans!

Step 1
Place the graham crackers in a large resealable bag and use a rolling pin to crush all of the crackers until they look like bread crumbs.

Step 2
Combine the melted butter with the graham cracker crumbs in a mixing bowl. Mix well.

Step 3
Spoon a tablespoon of graham cracker crumbs into each mini muffin cup.

Step 4
Use your fingers to press the bottom and the sides so that you form a mini crust in each muffin cup. Place in the freezer for 10 minutes.

Step 5
Meanwhile, combine the whipped cream cheese, peanut butter and powdered sugar in a bowl and mix until smooth. Place the mixture in a piping bag, or a resealable bag with one corner removed.

Step 6
Carefully squeeze a dollop of your peanut butter mixture into each mini crust.

Step 7
Place in the freezer for 5 minutes.

Step 8
After 5 minutes, drizzle each filled crust with the melted chocolate. Return to the freezer for another 5 minutes.

Step 9
Pop all of the crusts out of the muffin cups and enjoy!

 +  = **A Boosted Immune System !**

Mango   **Pomegranate**

Our *Mango Magic Salad* (page 84) will keep you healthy and active!

 +  = **Stronger Muscles !**

Kale   **Lemon**

Crispy Kale (page 85) will help your muscles stay strong and energized all day!

 +  = **Lots of Vitamin C !**

Strawberries   **Spinach**

Spectacular Spinach Salad (page 86) is full of vitamin C!

 +  = **Strong Bones !**

Apples   **Grapes**

WOW! *Waldorf Salad* (page 87) brings these fantastic fruits together in one super dish!

 + = **A Healthy Heart !**

Tomatoes   **Olive Oil**

Our *Tasty Tomato Tart* (page 88) will help keep your heart strong and healthy!

SUPERFOOD COMBINATIONS

Mango Magic Salad
Crispy Kale
Spectacular Spinach Salad
WOW! Waldorf Salad
Tasty Tomato Tart

Mango Magic Salad

PREP: 10 minutes
SERVINGS: 6

Ingredients

1 tablespoon honey
¼ cup lemon juice
2 mangos, sliced
1 mandarin orange, segmented
1 green apple, sliced
1 pineapple, cored and chopped
½ cup lychees in syrup, drained
½ cup pomegranate seeds
3 tablespoons shredded coconut

Tools

large bowl
rubber spatula
measuring spoons
measuring cup

Step 1

Combine the honey and lemon juice in a large bowl. Mix well.

Step 2

Add all the fruit to the honey mixture and toss until well coated; reserve a few mango slices to top your salad.

Step 3

Top with shredded coconut and the reserved mango slices.

Fun Fact !

Combining mangos rich in vitamin C with the super antioxidants found in pomegranates improves your body's immune system!

Crispy Kale

PREP: 25 minutes
SERVINGS: 4

Ingredients

2 bunches kale, washed and dried
3 tablespoons olive oil
¼ cup lemon juice
¼ cup Parmesan cheese
kosher salt

Tools

large mixing bowl
baking sheet
cutting board
knife
measuring spoons
measuring cup

Step 1
Preheat the oven to 300°F.

Step 2
Tear the kale leaves from the stems and chop the leaves.

Step 3
Place the chopped leaves in a bowl and drizzle with the olive oil and lemon juice. Toss until the kale leaves are fully coated. Season with salt.

Step 4
Lay the kale in a single layer on a baking sheet and top with the Parmesan cheese.

Step 5
Bake for 20 minutes or until crispy.

Fun Fact !

Combining iron-rich foods like kale with lemons that are high in vitamin C helps to keep your muscles from getting tired!

Spectacular Spinach Salad

Ingredients

Dressing:

1 shallot, chopped
2 tablespoons white balsamic vinegar
4 tablespoons olive oil
1 teaspoon sugar
¼ cup lemon juice
2 teaspoons thyme, chopped
salt to taste
2 pink peppercorns

Salad:

3 cups baby spinach
½ cup chopped basil
2 cups strawberries, halved

Tools

mini food processor
measuring spoons
measuring cup
large bowl
salad forks

PREP: 15 minutes
SERVINGS: 4-6

Step 1

Mix the shallot, vinegar, olive oil, sugar, lemon juice, thyme, salt and pink peppercorns in a mini food processor and process until smooth.

Step 2

Combine the spinach, basil and strawberries in a large bowl.

Step 3

Pour the dressing over the salad and toss to mix.

Strawberries and spinach are full of vitamin C, which may help wounds heal faster!

WOW! Waldorf Salad

PREP: 10 minutes
COOKING: 1 hour
SERVINGS: 4-6

Ingredients

1 cantaloupe
¼ cup fat-free mayonnaise
¼ cup lemon juice
3 apples, peeled, cored and diced
3 sticks celery, diced
1 cup arugula
¼ cup red grapes, halved
¼ cup walnuts, chopped

Tools

melon baller
large bowl
whisk
rubber spatula
measuring spoons
measuring cup

Step 1

Cut the cantaloupe in half and remove all of the seeds. Use a melon baller to scoop the cantaloupe into small balls. Set aside.

Step 2

Combine the fat-free mayonnaise and lemon juice in a bowl and mix well.

Step 3

Add the apples and celery to the mayonnaise mixture and toss to coat.

Step 4

Refrigerate for 1 hour.

Step 5

Serve over the arugula and top with the cantaloupe, grapes and walnuts.

Tasty Tomato Tart

PREP: 10 minutes
COOKING: 35 minutes
SERVINGS: 6-8

Ingredients

nonstick cooking spray
1 refrigerated pastry dough
1 cup shredded mozzarella cheese
15 basil leaves
5 tomatoes, cut into slices
2 teaspoons Italian herb blend
¼ cup olive oil
salt and pepper

Tools

tart pan
fork
measuring spoons
measuring cup

Step 1

Preheat the oven to 400°F.

Step 2

Spray a tart pan with nonstick cooking spray.

Step 3

Line the tart pan with the pastry dough. Use a fork to prick small holes all over the bottom of the pastry dough.

Step 4

Sprinkle half of the mozzarella cheese on top of the pastry layer.

Step 5

Layer 5 basil leaves on top of the cheese.

Step 6

Layer half of the tomato slices over the top.

Step 7

Sprinkle with half of the Italian herb mix, olive oil, salt and pepper.

Step 8

Repeat steps 4, 5, 6 and 7.

Step 9

Bake for 35 minutes or until the crust is golden brown.

Step 10

Garnish with the remaining basil leaves.

My Recipe!

10 up modsses

2 cup Butt

3 cup shugr

1 egg

Index

Apples
Caramel Apples - 24
Icc Cream Cone Cakes - 68
Mango Magic Salad - 84
Mini Gooey Apple Cakes - 11
My Little Roasted Hens - 53
Stuffed Apples - 19
WOW! Waldorf Salad - 87

Berries
Cheesecake Parfait - 75
Chewy Fruity Squares - 30
Fruity Breakfast Lollipops - 21
Mountaintop Strawberries - 29
Spectacular Spinach Salad - 86
Strawberry Field Dressing - 63

Carrots
Baked Egg Rolls - 36
Mix-It-Up Salad - 45
Pocket Chicken Salad - 42
Sticky Carrots - 33

Cheese
Banana Cupcakes - 72
Caramel Apples - 24
Cheesecake Parfait - 75
Chicken and Veggie Lasagna - 56
Crispy Kale - 85
Crunchy Chickpeas - 27
Famous Star Ravioli - 50
Fruity Breakfast Lollipops - 21
Tasty Tomato Tart - 88
Vegetable Quiches - 39
Veggie Quesadillas - 47

Chocolate
Cheesecake Parfait - 75
Chocolate Peanut Butter Cups - 81
Mountaintop Strawberries - 29

Cookies
Surprise Cookies - 77

Dressings *see also* Berries; Fruit
A Little Bit of Apricot - 64
A Touch of France Vinaigrette - 64
Asian Sensation - 65
Strawberry Field Dressing - 63
Sunflower Power Vinaigrette - 62
Zesty Mexican Vinaigrette - 60

Eggs
Breakfast Flowers - 8
Olé! A Spanish Tortilla - 13
Vegetable Quiches - 39

Fish & Seafood
Herby Salmon - 54
Slow Down for Gumbo - 59

Fruit *see also* Apples; Berries; Vegetarian
A Little Bit of Apricot - 64
Banana Cupcakes - 72
BBQ at Lunchtime - 41
Chewy Fruity Squares - 30
Fruity Breakfast Lollipops - 21
Ice Cream Cone Cakes - 68
Mango Magic Salad - 84
Mix-It-Up Salad - 45
Mountaintop Strawberries - 29
My Little Roasted Hens - 53
Spectacular Spinach Salad - 86
Strawberry Field Dressing - 63
Stuffed Apples - 19
To-Go Breakfast Pastries - 15
WOW! Waldorf Salad - 87

Greens
Crispy Kale - 85
Mix-It-Up Salad - 45
Pocket Chicken Salad - 42
Spectacular Spinach Salad - 86
Vegetable Quiches – 39
Veggie Quesadillas - 47
WOW! Waldorf Salad - 87

Herbs

Basil
A Little Bit of Apricot - 64
Chicken and Veggie Lasagna - 56
Famous Star Ravioli - 50
Tasty Tomato Tart - 88

Cilantro
Baked Egg Rolls - 36
Zesty Mexican Vinaigrette - 60

Parsley
Herby Salmon - 54
My Little Roasted Hens - 53

Rosemary
Crunchy Chickpeas - 27

Thyme
Spectacular Spinach Salad - 86
Sunflower Power Vinaigrette - 62
Vegetable Quiches - 39

Maple Syrup

Caramel Apples - 24
Fruity Breakfast Lollipops - 21
Mini Gooey Apple Cakes - 11

Nuts

Caramel Apples - 24
Cheesecake Parfait - 75
Famous Star Ravioli - 50
Mini Gooey Apple Cakes - 11
Mix-It-Up Salad - 45
My Little Roasted Hens - 53
WOW! Waldorf Salad - 87

Pasta

Chicken and Veggie Lasagna - 56
Famous Star Ravioli - 50

Pastry

To-Go Breakfast Pastries - 15
Fruity Breakfast Lollipops - 21

Peanut Butter

Chocolate Peanut Butter Cups - 81
Stuffed Apples - 19

Pork

Olé! A Spanish Tortilla - 13
Slow Down for Gumbo - 59

Poultry

Chicken
Baked Egg Rolls - 36
BBQ at Lunchtime - 41
Chicken and Veggie Lasagna - 56
Famous Star Ravioli - 50
Pocket Chicken Salad - 42
Mix-It-Up Salad - 45
Slow Down for Gumbo - 59

Cornish game hens
My Little Roasted Hens - 53

Turkey
Breakfast Flowers - 8

Tomatoes

BBQ at Lunchtime - 41
Breakfast Flowers - 8
Chicken and Veggie Lasagna - 56
Famous Star Ravioli - 50
Mix-It-Up Salad - 45
Olé! A Spanish Tortilla - 13
Pocket Chicken Salad - 42
Slow Down for Gumbo - 59
Tasty Tomato Tart - 88
Vegetable Quiches – 39
Veggie Quesadillas - 47

Vegetarian

Caramel Apples - 24
Cheesecake Parfait - 75
Chewy Fruity Squares - 30
Crispy Kale - 85
Crunchy Chickpeas - 27
Fruity Breakfast Lollipops - 21
Mango Magic Salad - 84
Mountaintop Strawberries - 29
Spectacular Spinach Salad - 86
Sticky Carrots - 33
Stuffed Apples - 19
Tasty Tomato Tart - 88
To-Go Breakfast Pastries - 15
Vegetable Quiches - 39
Veggie Quesadillas - 47
WOW! Waldorf Salad - 87

Wonton Wrappers

Baked Egg Rolls - 36
Famous Star Ravioli - 50

Recipe Index

A Little Bit of Apricot - 64
A Touch of France Vinaigrette - 64
Asian Sensation - 65

Baked Egg Rolls - 36
Banana Cupcakes - 72
BBQ at Lunchtime - 41
Breakfast Flowers - 8

Caramel Apples - 24
Cheesecake Parfait - 75
Chewy Fruity Squares - 30
Chicken and Veggie Lasagna - 56
Chocolate Peanut Butter Cups - 81
Crispy Kale - 85
Crunchy Chickpeas - 27

Famous Star Ravioli - 50
Fruity Breakfast Lollipops - 21

Herby Salmon - 54

Ice Cream Cone Cakes - 68

Mango Magic Salad - 84
Mini Gooey Apple Cakes - 11
Mix-It-Up Salad - 45

Mountaintop Strawberries - 29
My Little Roasted Hens - 53
Olé! A Spanish Tortilla - 13

Pocket Chicken Salad - 42

Slow Down for Gumbo - 59
Spectacular Spinach Salad - 86
Sticky Carrots - 33
Strawberry Field Dressing - 63
Stuffed Apples - 19
Sunflower Power Vinaigrette - 62
Surprise Cookies - 77

Tasty Tomato Tart - 88
To-Go Breakfast Pastries - 15

Vegetable Quiches - 39
Veggie Quesadillas - 47

WOW! Waldorf Salad - 87

Zesty Mexican Vinaigrette - 60

Kitchen Measurements

Dry

pinch = about 1/8 teaspoon

3 teaspoons = 1 tablespoon

4 tablespoons = 1/4 cup

16 tablespoons = 1 cup

2 cups = 1 pint

Liquid

1 tablespoon = 1/2 ounce

2 ounces = 1/4 cup

8 ounces = 1 cup

16 ounces = 2 cups or 1 pint

32 ounces = 1 quart

3 cups = 1 pint

2 pints = 1 quart

4 quarts = 1 gallon

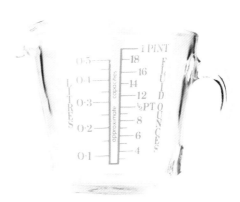

Twice As Good is a cooking show featuring twin sisters Hadley and Delaney. With creative and tasty dishes, the show encourages nutritious cooking and healthy eating in kids and parents alike. The show debuted in 2012 with its first season airing on various PBS/public television stations across the country. *Twice As Good's* second season is airing on PBS/public television stations in 2014. Season Three is scheduled to air in 2015.

For more information about the show and additional recipes, please visit **www.twiceasgoodshow.com**.

The Twice As Good Foundation supports nutrition and kid-focused charities. Each year the Twice As Good Foundation distributes 5 percent of its 12-quarter rated average value to charities supporting kids and nutrition.

Organizations the Foundation Supports

HARVARD MEDICAL SCHOOL,
DIVISION OF NUTRITION

STANFORD SCHOOL OF MEDICINE,
PREVENTION RESEARCH CENTER,
NUTRITION STUDIES RESEARCH GROUP

JOE DIMAGGIO CHILDREN'S HOSPITAL

ST. JUDE CHILDREN'S
RESEARCH HOSPITAL

JUVENILE DIABETES
RESEARCH FOUNDATION

PAN-MASS CHALLENGE BENEFITING
THE DANA-FARBER CANCER INSTITUTE

Acknowledgements

Our thanks to those who have made this cookbook possible!

Recipes & Food Styling: Elizabeth Bouza

Elizabeth is a Miami-based chef who develops recipes and serves as the food stylist for *Twice as Good*. Inspired by her father to cook, this project has been a labor of love.

Photography: Karin Martinez

Karin is a South Florida-based photographer who has been shooting kids, families and weddings for over 15 years. Her work can be viewed at www.karinmartinez.com.

Branding & Logos: Audrey Denson

Audrey is an award-winning graphic designer, internet, branding and creative image specialist for corporate, non-profit and small business clients throughout the U.S.

Layout/Graphic Design: Grace Delanoy

Grace is a creative communications specialist who combines her writing, design, photography and marketing skills to support authors, equestrian- and wellness-oriented clients.